Abraham Lincoln's Dueling Words

To Chris, who knows a lot about breaking up fights and keeping the peace—
all while encouraging a moody writer.

And to all readers who learn from their own mistakes.

—D. J. B.

To Dave Hanson, a model model.

—S. S.

Published by
PEACHTREE PUBLISHERS
1700 Chattahoochee Avenue
Atlanta, Georgia 30318-2112
www.peachtree-online.com

Text © 2018 Donna Janell Bowman
Illustrations © 2018 S. D. Schindler

Edited by Kathy Landwehr
Design and composition by Nicola Simmonds Carmack

The illustrations were rendered in watercolor and ink.

Printed in October 2017 by Tien Wah, Malaysia
10 9 8 7 6 5 4 3 2 1
First Edition
ISBN 978-1-56145-852-3

Library of Congress Cataloging-in-Publication Data

Names: Bowman, Donna Janell, author. | Schindler, S. D., illustrator.
Title: Abraham Lincoln's dueling words / written by Donna Janell Bowman ;
illustrated by S. D. Schindler.
Description: First edition. | Atlanta GA : Peachtree Publishers, 2018. | Audience: Age 6–10.
Audience: Grade K to 3.
Identifiers: LCCN 2017012684 | ISBN 9781561458523
Subjects: LCSH: Lincoln, Abraham, 1809–1865—Juvenile literature. | Shields, James, 1806–1879—
Juvenile literature. | Presidents—United States—Biography—Juvenile literature. | Dueling—United
States—History—19th century—Juvenile literature.
Classification: LCC E457.35 .B69 2018 | DDC 973.7092 [B] —dc23 LC record available at
https://lccn.loc.gov/2017012684

Abraham Lincoln's Dueling Words

Donna Janell Bowman
Illustrated by S. D. Schindler

"It has been my experience that folks who have no vices

have very few virtues."

—*Abraham Lincoln*

PEACHTREE
ATLANTA

See those two fellows in the boat, looking all grim and serious? Maybe you recognize one of them from your history books.

Yep, that's Abraham Lincoln, Springfield's favorite joke-telling, story-spinning, honest-to-the-bone lawyer.

Lincoln did something to make that other fellow James Shields as mad as a badger. Yessir, he got himself into a heap of trouble.

Now this boat is headed to Bloody Island, where nothing good ever happens. And Shields is fuming over those long, shiny, razor-sharp swords.

Before we jump ahead to something frightful, you might be wondering what got Lincoln into this scrape in the first place.

Back in Springfield, folks knew Lincoln for his top-hatted head full of smarts, but also for his friendliness and knee-slapping tales. Any little ol' thing could start a story spinning in his mind. Even in court, which should have been quiet and businesslike, something might tickle his funny bone.

"That brings to mind a story," he would begin. Often, his homespun tale would sway the jury to his side. Sometimes, the judge even busted out laughing.

"If I did not laugh," Lincoln said, "I would die."

But Lincoln was also a timber of a man who could best almost anyone in a just-for-fun wrestling match. All those years of swinging an axe and splitting rails made him strong as a mule. Now, as a young lawyer, he mostly wrestled with his own stubborn streak.

James Shields was a hot-tempered, well-educated Irishman with a knack for arguing. Everyone knew he was a crack shot with a pistol. He was only fifteen years old when he was challenged to his first duel. It's a good thing the gunpowder was wet that day, or one of them might have been pushing up daisies.

Shields soldiered in the Black Hawk War, just like Lincoln.

He became a Springfield lawyer, just like Lincoln.

And he served in the Illinois Legislature, just like Lincoln.

But unlike Lincoln, Shields was known for his arrogance and his serious side. Some folks thought there wasn't a joke-telling, story-spinning bone in his body.

Our story begins in the summer of 1842. Lincoln was growing his law practice and supporting the Whigs, the political party he belonged to. Shields was the Illinois state auditor, which is a fancy title for someone who keeps track of the state budget and taxes. He was 100 percent loyal to the Democrats, the opposing party.

Yep, Lincoln and Shields were political competitors.

Now, Illinois and its State Banks were in a financial crisis and lots of poor folks lost their life savings. Lincoln and Shields disagreed about how to fix the problem. Then Shields, along with the governor and treasurer, signed a proclamation that ordered folks to pay their taxes with silver or gold instead of bank dollars.

Lincoln read the proclamation and paced the floor. This new requirement would hurt poor folks more than ever! Was Shields even thinking about them?

Then again, he thought, maybe there was a way that the proclamation could make the Whigs look good.

A rascally idea needled its way into Lincoln's mind and he stitched a political plan.

If you've been waiting for that moment when he got himself into trouble, here it comes.

Lincoln scratched out a letter to the editor of the *Sangamo Journal*, the local Whig newspaper. He signed the letter from a made-up character named Aunt Rebecca, from a made-up place called the Lost Townships. Words like *'spose* and *reckon* and *finickin about*—words Lincoln had used as a backwoods kid—flew across the page.

The letter was silly.

It was clever.

It was a great big mistake!

In Lincoln's letter, Aunt Rebecca fussed about the state proclamation. She griped about the Democrats. And she called James Shields a fool, a liar, and a "conceity dunce." Just like that, Lincoln's political jab turned into a personal attack.

The next day, the whole town read Aunt Rebecca's letter in the newspaper.

A few days later, Lincoln's sweetheart, Mary Todd, and her friend, Julia Jayne, giggled over the letter.

Wouldn't you know it, they decided to write their own letter. And they signed it from Aunt Rebecca too.

Mary and Julia's letter was also printed in the newspaper.

Then another Aunt Rebecca letter appeared.

Each letter poked fun at Shields. Imagine opening up the newspaper and reading spiteful things about yourself again and again.

Shields was insulted.

He was offended.

He was fighting MAD!

Shields sent a friend to the editor's office to find out who wrote the Aunt Rebecca letters.

As soon as Lincoln heard about the demand, he told the editor to give one name: Abraham Lincoln.

Now Shields had someone to blame.

Letters flew back and forth between the men.

Shields accused Lincoln of damaging his character, his reputation, and his honor. He demanded a public apology.

I reckon Lincoln felt offended too. Shields had accused him of writing all of the letters, but that wasn't true.

"You have made assumptions without stopping to inquire whether I really am the author," Lincoln wrote to Shields. "I cannot submit to answer your note any further until your accusation is withdrawn."

Hold on now. I know what you're thinking. Why didn't Lincoln fess up about what he had done—and what he hadn't?

Well, in those long ago times, there were rules for gentlemanly conduct—proper ways of doing things. Lincoln thought that Shields wasn't following the rules.

Shields wouldn't budge. He wanted an apology.

Lincoln wouldn't budge. He wanted Shields to ask like a gentleman.

Instead, Shields challenged Lincoln to a duel.

If Lincoln refused the challenge, he would be viewed as a coward. People would lose respect for him.

But dueling was illegal in Illinois. If Lincoln and Shields were caught, they could both go to prison. Or be kicked out of public service for life. Or one of them could even land himself in the grave.

"I did not want to kill Shields," Lincoln later said. "And, furthermore, I didn't want the fellow to kill me."

There was no guarantee that he could win a duel with Shields.

If Lincoln had to fight, he would have to be smart.

A glance in the mirror might have given him a lifesaving idea.

As the challenged man, Lincoln got to decide the rules of the duel. Most duels were fought with pistols, but he had a sharper idea. Lincoln spelled out his terms.

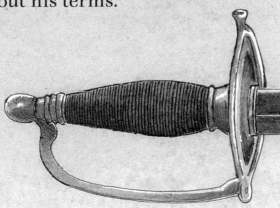

1st. Weapons—Cavalry broadswords of the largest size.

2nd. Position—A plank ten feet long, & from nine to twelve inches broad to be firmly fixed on edge, on the ground, as the line between us which neither is to pass his foot over upon forfeit of his life. Next a line drawn on the ground on either side of said plank & parallel with it, each at the distance of the whole length of the sword and three feet additional from the plank; and the passing of his own such line by either party during the fight shall be deemed a surrender of the contest.

Only a man with unusual strength could wrangle such a long sword.

Only a tall man with very long arms could reach his opponent from that distance.

And only a man with a sense of humor could come up with such ridiculous terms.

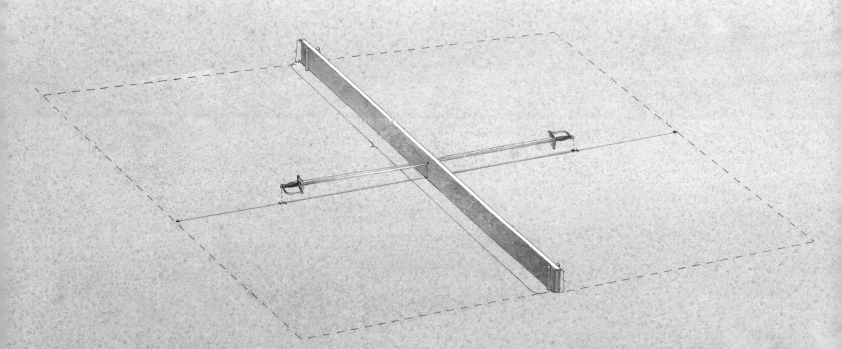

If you're feeling squeamish or worrisome, hold on to your seats. Because here we are on Bloody Island—right back where we started—smack dab in the middle of the Mississippi River.

Our two stubborn fellows make their way to the field of honor, where the duel will take place.

Lincoln looks mighty regretful. He wishes he'd never written that Rebecca letter.

The seconds have prepared the field according to Lincoln's terms.

What's a second, you ask? Well, if there was a duel dictionary, "second" would mean assistant. The seconds are responsible for managing the duel, but their main job is to prevent the duel if possible. If they fail, blood will be spilled.

Shields slashes the air with his broadsword, warming up for the fight. His second begs him to back down.

Shields refuses.

Before you turn the page, you might want to cover your eyes.

Folks have crowded the banks to watch. The two men step forward.

Shields struts and paces, eager to begin. Lincoln raises his sword high, high, higher. He slices a large branch from a very tall tree. If Shields sees how far Lincoln can reach, maybe he'll reconsider.

But Shields doesn't flinch.

Oh my! What do you suppose Lincoln will do now?

Stop!

The seconds jump between Lincoln and Shields and call a delay. They huddle together and hatch a plan.

They tell Lincoln that Shields has withdrawn his accusation.

Lincoln doesn't know it's a fib. But now, according to the gentleman's code, he can explain what he did—and why. And he does the most important thing.

Lincoln apologizes.

"I did write the Lost Township letter," Lincoln says. "I wrote that wholly for political effect. I had no intention of injuring your personal or private character."

Shields accepts Lincoln's apology. Both sides agree that all honor has been restored.

Whew! You can uncover your eyes now.

Swords are sheathed.

Hands are shaken.

The almost-duel is over.

You can bet a shiny copper penny that Abraham Lincoln's great big mistake teaches him to be a better man.

It's a good thing, too, because years from now there will be a different kind of proclamation to defend. A different kind of battle to fight. A different reason to be civil. When that day comes, Lincoln and Shields will decide to work together.

"If all the good things I have ever done are remembered as long and as well as my scrape with Shields, it is plain I shall not soon be forgotten."

—Abraham Lincoln

Abraham Lincoln's Almost-Duel

You might be asking yourself how come you've never heard of Lincoln's almost-duel. Truth be told, he was ashamed of it. Lincoln called it the meanest thing he had ever done. He vowed never again to write a hurtful word or use another man for political gain. Lincoln was changed. Six weeks after the duel, when Abraham Lincoln and Mary Todd married, they agreed to keep this story to themselves forever.

Mudslinging through the Printed Word

In the nineteenth-century, politicians frequently resorted to mudslinging, which means they publicly attacked the reputation of other candidates or opponents. Often they did this through anonymous or pseudonymous (signed with a fake name) letters and stories published in newspapers.

Scholars believe that Lincoln wrote many such pieces, even before the Aunt Rebecca letters. In 1837, he wrote a series of letters signed "Sampson's Ghost," which lampooned a lawyer who Lincoln believed had stolen land from his client.

The Aunt Rebecca Letters

Lincoln wasn't the only person to write a letter signed Aunt Rebecca. He wasn't even the first. In all, there were four such letters, published between August 19 and September 9, 1842. Lincoln admitted to writing the second letter, published September 2.

Each letter was meant to sound like it was written by the same author, but Lincoln's skilled comic dialect and satire stand out. Scholars who have studied the style, diction, grammar, and dialect of all the letters came up with reasonable assumptions about their authorship. The first and third letters were likely written by Simeon Francis, the editor of the *Sangamo Journal*. Mary Todd probably wrote the fourth letter and a silly poem with the help of Julia Jayne.

Today, the only surviving note related to the almost-duel is Lincoln's handwritten note to his second, Dr. Merryman, that spells out the terms of the duel.

James Shields

James Shields was born in Ireland in 1806. He immigrated to the United States in the 1820s and first worked at sea. He then worked as a fencing (sword fighting) instructor and as a school teacher before studying law and settling in Illinois.

Though his contemporaries considered Shields a vain and arrogant man, he led a long and impressive political and military career after the almost-duel. Among other accomplishments, he served as governor of the Oregon Territory, and he remains the only US senator to have represented three states: Illinois, Minnesota, and Missouri. During the Civil War, Lincoln appointed Shields Brigadier-General.

Shields was five feet nine inches tall—seven inches shorter than Abraham Lincoln.

The Illinois Banking Crisis

At the time of the 1842 almost-duel, the United States was suffering through a great financial depression. People didn't trust the banks or the government. Wages were down, prices were elevated, unemployment was rampant, and people couldn't pay back their bank loans.

There was no unified American currency as there is today. Instead, individual banks printed their own paper money (bank notes) that was backed by silver and gold coins (specie), produced by the US government. One bank's currency was worth less at competing banks.

By 1837, the State Bank of Illinois was on the brink of collapse. Many people withdrew all their state money—which quickly became almost worthless. In early 1842, Shields, along with the Illinois governor and treasurer (all Democrats), signed a proclamation demanding payment of taxes and school debts with specie. People were furious. And broke.

The Whigs viewed the proclamation as an indication that state officials were more concerned with their own salaries than the welfare of the citizens. They were poised to attack and Abraham Lincoln was prepared to lead the charge with his Rebecca letter.

In 1863, while Abraham Lincoln was president, Congress approved the National Banking system, which was followed by the Federal Reserve Act that evolved into our current financial system.

About Writing This Book

In 2012, I stumbled upon a one-sentence mention of Lincoln's duel that floored me. The more I researched, the more I realized that Lincoln was a regular guy who made lots of mistakes—just like the rest of us. I worried about whether I should share this less-than-stellar event from his life, until I came across a recollection by his former law partner William Herndon. After reading a biography, Lincoln complained that the writer "magnifies his perfections, and suppresses his imperfections." Lincoln ended his rant by stating that biographies of the day "commemorate a lie and cheat posterity out of the truth." I took that as permission from Lincoln himself to tell the story of his duel. After all, how he responded to his great big mistake made him a better man.

Lincoln never wrote or spoke about the almost-duel. In fact, during the Civil War—more than twenty years after the event—an Army officer asked Lincoln if rumors about the duel were true. Lincoln replied, "I do not deny it, but if you desire my friendship you will never mention it again."

Thankfully, history hasn't forgotten that our most revered president—the great emancipator—was a regular guy who learned from his mistakes.

See for Yourself!

Transcripts of the Rebecca letters
Collected Works of Abraham Lincoln, the Abraham Lincoln Association
quod.lib.umich.edu/l/lincoln/lincoln1/1:310?rgn=div1;view=fulltext

Lincoln's letter to Merryman with duel instructions
Abraham Lincoln Papers, the Library of Congress
www.memory.loc.gov/cgi-bin/ampage?collId=mal&fileName=mal1/000/0003800/malpage.db&recNum=0

Issues of the *Sangamo Journal*
Illinois Digital Newspaper Collections
idnc.library.illinois.edu/cgi-bin/illinois?a=d&d=SJO18420909.2.162&srpos=4&e=-------en-20--1--txt-txIN-Letter+from+the+Lost+townships

For full bibliography, sources for all quotations, and expanded information visit
www.donnajanellbowman.com.